God's Love for Us and His Remedy for Our Sins

Al Matlock

TEACH Services, Inc.
P U B L I S H I N G
www.TEACHServices.com • (800) 367-1844

Jackfish Lake, Ontario, Canada, where I have spent many hours and days fishing and enjoying God's creation.

A special thanks to:

Carol Matlock

Pastor Throstur Thordarson

Becky Matlock

Jackie Vander Heyden

Dave Yancey

For encouragement, information, and assistance in the writing of these words.

Be true to yourself, seeking God and His love and mercy, and allow His Word to be your guide.

And this is love, that we walk after his commandments. This is the commandment, That, as ye have heard from the beginning, ye should walk in it. (2 John 1:6)

Introduction

Before we begin this study of God's love and laws, I would like to tell you a little about myself. I was one of nine children, raised by a very devout Christian mother (my father was not converted until many years later). She lived what she believed and did her best to teach her children to do the same. When I was young, it seemed less important and more of a nuisance, but her love for her children and her God persevered, and she never gave up.

As I grew older, I began to think more about God and my salvation, but I had a big problem in my mind. My mother taught us to worship on Saturday, while just about everybody else worshipped on Sunday. This bothered me much, as I didn't know anybody in my early years who kept Saturday as a holy day except my mother. So, as a result, out of respect to my mother, I attended a Sabbath-keeping church for several years before I felt the urge to find out why I was going to church on Saturday instead of Sunday. I began some studies provided by the church and was convinced that the seventh-day Sabbath was what God had blessed and made holy for a day of rest each week.

Then one day, I was visiting with my niece, and she asked me why Grandma (my mother) went to church on Saturday instead of Sunday. Even though I had given enough study to convince myself, I couldn't give a good answer. This bothered me a lot because the Bible says, *"But sanctify the Lord God in your hearts: and be ready always to give an answer to every man that asketh you a reason of the hope that is in you with meekness and fear" (1 Peter 3:15).*

Then began a long period of prayer and study to try to learn how to give an answer to my niece or anyone else who might ask. Thank you, Debra. I hope someday you have the opportunity to read this book and get the answer to your question to me from many years ago.

A Study of God's Love and Laws

Let's consider God's love, God's laws, Jewish laws, and Moses' laws. Is there one law, or laws, that prevail above others? What was the first law, or laws, mentioned in the Bible?

In the concordance of my Bible, which is the *Authorized King James Version*, there are sixty-nine references to the word law. I know there are more because the first one I will refer to (not mentioned in the concordance) says, *"And I will make thy seed to multiply as the stars of heaven, and will give unto thy seed all these countries; and in thy seed shall all the nations of the earth be blessed; because that Abraham obeyed my voice, and kept*

> *Let's consider God's love, God's laws, Jewish laws, and Moses' laws.*

my charge, my commandments, my statutes, and my laws" (Gen. 26:4–5).

I have not found anything mentioned about laws and commandments before this, but these verses make it very clear that God's commandments existed long before they were given, written in stone, to Moses and the Israelites. It also makes it clear that He will bless *all* nations of the earth if they keep His commandments and His laws, not just the Jews and Israelites.

Here are some others to consider:

> *And he [Moses] cried unto the LORD; and the LORD shewed him a tree, which when he had cast into the waters, the waters were made sweet: there he made for them a statute and an ordinance, and there he proved them, And said, if thou wilt diligently harken to the voice of the LORD thy God, and wilt do that which is right in his sight, and wilt give ear to his commandments, and keep all his statutes, I will put none of these diseases upon thee, which I have brought upon the Egyptians: for I am the Lord that healeth thee. (Exod. 15:25–26)*

This was also before the commandments were given in stone.

Another passage that points directly to the fourth of the Ten Commandments, also before they were given in stone, is:

> *Then said the LORD unto Moses, Behold, I will rain bread from heaven for you; and the people shall go out and gather a certain rate every day, that I may prove them, whether they will walk in my law, or no. And it shall come to pass, that on the sixth day they*

shall prepare that which they bring in; and it shall be twice as much as they gather daily. (Exod. 16:4–5)

And they gathered it every morning, every man according to his eating: and when the sun waxed hot, it melted.

And it came to pass, that on the sixth day they gathered twice as much bread [manna], two omers for one man: and all the rulers of the congregation came and told Moses. And he said unto them, this is that which the LORD hath said, to morrow is the rest of the holy sabbath unto the LORD: bake that which ye will bake to day, and seethe that ye will seethe; and that which remaineth over lay up for you to be kept until the morning. And they laid it up till the morning, as Moses bade: and it did not stink, neither was there any worm therein. And Moses said, Eat that to day; for to day is a sabbath unto the LORD: to day ye shall not find it in the field. Six days ye shall gather it; but on the seventh day, which is the sabbath, in it there shall be none. And it came to pass, that there went out some of the people on the seventh day for to gather, and they found none.

And the LORD said unto Moses, how long refuse ye to keep my commandments and my laws? See, for that the LORD hath given you the sabbath, therefore He giveth you on the sixth day the bread of two days; abide ye every man in his place, let no man go out of his place on the seventh day. So the people rested on the seventh day. (Exod. 16:21–30)

This gives us a pretty definite picture of the fact that God's laws were established at the beginning. These verses state plainly that the keeping of the Sabbath (fourth commandment of the ten written in stone) was part of the law from the beginning.

So many times, I hear people say that when Jesus died for our sins, the law was nailed to the cross and is no longer necessary. Granted, there were laws that were abolished, but were all of God's laws nailed to the cross? No! The laws that were abolished were mainly the sacrificial laws, which were no longer needed since Jesus made the ultimate sacrifice for all of us.

At this point let's see exactly what the Ten Commandments say:

Thou shalt have no other gods before me.

Thou shalt not make unto thee any graven image, or any likeness of any thing that is in heaven above, or that is in the earth beneath, or that is in the water under the earth. Thou shalt not bow down thyself to them, nor serve them: for I the Lord thy God am a jealous God, visiting the iniquity of the fathers upon the children unto the third and fourth generation of them that hate me; and shewing mercy unto thousands of them that love me, and keep my commandments.

Thou shalt not take the name of the LORD thy God in vain; for the LORD will not hold him guiltless that taketh His name in vain.

<u>REMEMBER</u> the sabbath day, to keep it holy. Six days shalt thou labour, and do all thy work: but the seventh day is the sabbath of the LORD thy God: in it thou shalt not do any work, thou, nor thy son, nor thy daughter, thy manservant, nor thy maidservant, nor thy cattle, nor thy stranger that is within thy gates: for in six days the LORD made heaven and earth, the sea, and all that in them is, and rested the seventh day: wherefore the LORD blessed the sabbath day, and hallowed it." [Reference Genesis 2:1–3: Thus the heavens and the earth were finished, and all the host of them. And on the seventh day God ended his work which he had made; and he rested on the seventh day from all his work which he had made. And God blessed the seventh day, and sanctified it: because that in it he had rested from all his work which God created and made.]

> **<u>REMEMBER</u> the sabbath day, to keep it holy.**

Honour thy father and thy mother: that thy days may be long upon the land which the LORD thy God giveth thee.

Thou shalt not kill.

Thou shalt not commit adultery.

Thou shalt not steal.

Thou shalt not bear false witness against thy neighbour.

Thou shalt not covet thy neighbour's house, thou shalt not covet thy neighbour's wife, nor his manservant, nor his maidservant, nor his ox, nor his ass, nor any thing that is thy neighbour's. (Exod. 20:3–17)

Did you ever hear the words, "It's not written in stone" or "It's written in stone?" These phrases indicate it may be permanent or law. The Ten Commandments written above are, of course, written in stone by God's own hand and meant to last forever. David said, *"Concerning thy testimonies [Ten Commandments], I have known of old that thou hast founded them for ever" (Ps. 119:152).*

Let's look at a few scriptures to verify if we should be keeping God's commandments today.

And the LORD spake unto Moses, saying, speak thou also unto the children of Israel, saying, Verily my sabbaths ye shall keep: for it is a sign between me and you throughout your generations; that ye may know that I am the LORD that doth sanctify you. Ye shall keep the sabbath therefore; for it is holy unto you: every one that defileth it shall surely be put to death: for whosoever doeth any work therein, that soul shall be cut off from among his people. Six days may work be done; but in the seventh is the sabbath of rest, holy to the LORD: whosoever doeth any work in the sabbath day, he shall surely be put to death. Wherefore the children of Israel shall keep the sabbath, to observe the sabbath throughout their generations, for a perpetual covenant. It is a sign between me and the children of Israel for ever: for in six days the LORD *made heaven and earth, and on the seventh day he rested, and was refreshed.*

And he gave unto Moses, when he had made an end of communing with him upon mount Sinai, two tables of testimony, tables of stone, written with the finger of God. (Exod. 31:12–18)

Two words in these verses leave no question about the Ten Commandments (God's laws) being valid today. They are: *perpetual*, defined by Webster's dictionary as everlasting, continual, eternal; and the word *forever*, defined by Webster's dictionary as for all time, always. Let's go all the way into the new earth.

16 *God's Love for Us and His Remedy for Our Sins*

> *For as the new heavens and the new earth, which I will make, shall remain before me, saith the LORD, so shall your seed and your name remain. And it shall come to pass, that from one new moon to another, and from one sabbath to another, shall all flesh come to worship before me, saith the LORD. (Isa. 66:22–23)*

Now, when God said *"All flesh shall come before me to worship,"* He was not speaking of just the Israelites, or Jews, but to everyone in the new earth. That means you and I will worship Him on the Sabbath day in the new earth.

Let's go back now to, *"Know therefore that the LORD thy God, he is God, the faithful God, which keepeth covenant and mercy with them that love him and keep His commandments to a thousand generations" (Deut. 7:9).*

Note that He said, "Them that love him and keep his commandments." Does that mean that just the Israelites love Him? I think not. It means just what it says. It means *all* that love and keep His commandments.

Okay. Here's a question for you. How long are a thousand generations? Let's do some math. Luke 3:23–38 lists the generations from Adam to Jesus. I counted seventy-six generations, including Jesus. Jesus was age thirty-three when He died, so wouldn't it be 1,984 years (written in 2017) from His death to the present? According to Bible history, those seventy-six generations took about 3,950 years. If you divide 3,950 by 76 generations, it comes to 51.9 years per generation. We have no record of how many generations there were from Jesus to the present time, but we do have a date of about 2,020 years after Jesus's death to the present.

Using those numbers and seventy years per generation (present life span?) makes another twenty-nine generations.

So, Adam to Jesus equals seventy-six generations, and Jesus to the present equals twenty-nine, giving us a total of one hundred five generations from creation to the present. One hundred five from one thousand equals 895 generations to go. That many generations times seventy years equals 61,650 years. Now, we know that in the New Earth, we will live forever, so if the Lord comes before another 895 generations, then that takes us to forever. Sounds like when God said forever and perpetual, that's exactly what He meant. Of course, we know that these numbers are not exact, but even several thousand years difference would still take us to forever. Let's add a few more.

The works of his hands are verity and judgment; all his commandments are sure. They stand fast for ever and ever, and are done in truth and uprightness. He sent redemption unto his people: he hath commanded His covenant for ever: holy and reverend is His name. The fear of the Lord is the beginning of wisdom: a good understanding have all they that do His commandments: his praise endureth forever. (Ps. 111:7–10)

Concerning thy testimonies, I have known of old that thou hast founded them for ever. (Ps. 119:152)

Salvation is far from the wicked: for they seek not thy statutes. (Ps. 119:155)

There is a way which seemeth right unto a man, but the end thereof are the ways of death. (Prov. 14:12)

18   *God's Love for Us and His Remedy for Our Sins*

We must be guided by what God's Word teaches us and not what seems right.

This verse is something to consider very seriously. We must be guided by what God's Word teaches us and not what seems right. For instance, it seems right to go to church and worship God on Sunday, but that is not what God's Word teaches. Now, to worship God on Sunday is good, as it is to worship God every day, but to use it as a holy day is wrong because God blessed the seventh day and made it holy, so that should be the day we keep holy, as God directed. Moving on with more verses:

He that keepeth the commandment keepeth his own soul; but he that despiseth his ways shall die. (Prov. 19:16)

They that forsake the law praise the wicked: but such as keep the law contend with them. Evil men understand not judgment: but they that seek the LORD understand all things. Better is the poor that walketh in his uprightness, than he that is perverse in his ways, though he be rich. Whoso keepeth the law is a wise son: but he that is a companion of riotous men shameth his father. He that by usury and unjust gain increaseth his substance, he shall gather it for him that will pity the poor. He that turneth away his ear from hearing the law, even his prayer shall be abomination. (Prov. 28:4–9)

The earth mourneth and fadeth away, the world languisheth and fadeth away, the haughty people of the earth do languish. The earth also is defiled under the inhabitants thereof; because they have transgressed the laws, changed the ordinance, broken the everlasting covenant. Therefore hath the curse devoured the earth, and they that dwell therein are desolate: therefore the inhabitants of the earth are burned, and few men left. (Isa. 24:4–6)

Why is the world in such a mess today? The verses above give us a pretty strong answer. Because "they have transgressed the laws, changed the ordinance (seventh-day Sabbath to Sunday), broken the everlasting covenant." Let's insert one single verse here. *"The grass withereth, the flower fadeth: but the word of our God shall stand for ever"* (Isa. 40:8).

What does that mean? Well, if we believe in God, then we should believe what it says, *"For I am the LORD, I change not"* (Mal. 3:6) and *"Jesus Christ the same yesterday, and to day, and for ever"* (Heb. 13:8).

It seems reasonable that since Jesus was with God from the beginning to forever, that there wouldn't be any changing from His original plan of commandments or laws for us today.

Here's an interesting verse, *"Therefore have I also made you contemptible and base before all the people, according as ye have not kept my ways, but have been partial in the law"* (Mal. 2:9).

I can see a good example of this verse as I visit and reason with friends from different religious denominations. Most believe we should keep the Ten Commandments, yet they still worship on Sunday and work or do their own thing on the true seventh-day Sabbath.

> *Most believe we should keep the Ten Commandments, yet they still worship on Sunday and work or do their own thing on the true seventh-day Sabbath.*

If ye fulfil the royal law according to the scripture, thou shalt love thy neighbor as thyself, ye do well: but if ye have respect to persons, ye commit sin, and are convinced of the law as transgressors. For whosoever shall keep the whole law, and yet offend in one point, he is guilty of all. For he that said, Do not commit adultery, said also, do not kill. Now if thou commit no adultery, yet if thou kill, thou art become a transgressor of the law. (James 2:8–11)

Just to reinforce the fact that God expects us to keep the Ten Commandments, here are some more verses that need to be taken into account. All are New Testament, this time.

Then came to Jesus scribes and Pharisees, which were of Jerusalem, saying, Why do thy disciples transgress the tradition of the elders? for they wash not their hands when they eat bread. But he answered and said unto them, Why do ye also transgress the commandment of God by your tradition? For God commanded, saying, Honour thy father and mother [fifth commandment]: and, he that curseth father or mother, let him die the death. But ye say, Whosoever shall say to his father or his mother, It is a gift, by whatsoever thou mightest be profited by me; and honour not his father or his mother, he shall be free. Thus have ye made the commandment of God of none effect by your tradition. Ye hypocrites, well did Esaias prophesy of you, saying, This people draweth nigh unto me with their mouth, and honoureth me with their lips; but their heart is far from me. But in vain they do worship me, teaching for doctrines the commandments of men. (Matt. 15:1–9)

And again,

He answered and said unto them, Well hath Esaias prophesied of you hypocrites, as it is written, this people honoureth me with their lips, but their heart is far from me. Howbeit in vain do they worship me, teaching for doctrines the commandments of men. For laying aside the commandment of God, ye hold the tradition of men, as the washing of pots and cups: and many other such like things ye do. And He said unto them, Full well ye reject the commandment of God, that ye may keep your own tradition. (Mark 7:6–9)

(Sorry folks, but Sunday worship is a tradition of man, not of God.)

And, behold, one came and said unto him, Good Master, what good thing shall I do, that I may have eternal life?

And he said unto him, Why callest thou me good? there is none good but one, that is, God: but if thou wilt enter into life, keep the commandments.

He saith unto him, Which?

Jesus said, Thou shalt do no murder [sixth commandment], thou shalt not commit adultery [seventh commandment], thou shall not steal [eighth commandment]. (Matt. 19:16–19)

I need to say right here, this is Jesus talking, and He is telling this man if he wants to be saved, to keep the commandments. He goes on to quote more. "Thou shalt not bear false witness [ninth commandment], Honour thy father and thy mother [fifth commandment]: and, Thou shalt love thy neighbor as thyself."

This last quote that Jesus made to the young man was not one of the Ten Commandments written in stone, but it reflects God's expectations of us concerning our fellow man, which all are our neighbors, according to the answer Jesus gave the lawyer:

This last quote that Jesus made to the young man reflects God's expectations of us concerning our fellow man.

And, behold, a certain lawyer stood up, and tempted him, saying, Master, what shall I do to inherit eternal life?

He said unto him, What is written in the law? How readest thou?

And he answering said, Thou shalt love the Lord thy God with all thy heart, and with all thy soul, and with all thy strength, and with all thy mind; and thy neighbour as thyself.

And he said unto him, Thou hast answered right: this do, and thou shalt live.

But he, willing to justify himself, said unto Jesus, And who is my neighbour?

And Jesus answering said, A certain man went down from Jerusalem to Jericho, and fell among thieves, which stripped him of his raiment, and wounded him, and departed, leaving him half dead. And by chance there came down a certain priest that way: and when he saw him, he passed by on the other side. And likewise a Levite, when he was at the place, came and looked on him, and passed by on the other side. But a certain Samaritan, as he journeyed, came where he was: and when he saw him, he had compassion on him, And went to him, and bound up his wounds, pouring in oil and wine, and set him on his own beast, and brought him to an inn, and took care of him. And on the morrow when he departed, he took out two pence, and gave them to the host, and said unto him, Take care of him; and whatsoever thou spendest more, when I come again, I will repay thee. Which now of these three, thinkest thou, was neighbour unto him that fell among the thieves?

And he said, He that showed mercy on him. Then said Jesus unto him, Go, and do thou likewise. (Luke 10:25–37)

This shows that all people are our neighbors whether we know them or not.

And Jesus answered him, the first of all the commandments is, Hear, O Israel; the Lord our God is one Lord: and thou shalt love the Lord thy God with all thy heart, and with all thy soul, and with all thy mind, and with all thy strength: this is the first commandment. And the second is like, namely this, thou shall love thy neighbour as thyself There is none other commandment greater than these. (Mark 12:29–31)

So, the first four of the Ten Commandments show our duty to God, and the last six show our duty to man.

More verses from the New Testament:

Jesus said, Think not that I come to destroy the law, or the prophets: I am not come to destroy, but to fulfil. For verily I say unto you, till heaven and earth pass, one jot or one tittle shall in no wise pass from the law, till all be fulfilled. Whosoever therefore shall break one of these least commandments, and shall teach men so, he shall be called the least in the kingdom of heaven: but whosoever shall do and teach them, the same shall be called great in the kingdom of heaven. (Matt. 5:17–19)

Verse 18 says, *"one jot or one tittle shall in no wise pass from the law, till all be fulfilled."* Some say when Jesus died, He fulfilled all. Those folks must not have read the first part of that verse. It plainly says, *"Till heaven and earth pass."* Guess what? Heaven and earth are still here and will be till God makes them new again. And even more important, is the definition of the word *fulfilled*. Check it out.

Webster's definition of "fulfill":

ful•fill, ful•fil (ful-f*il*)

v. [-filled; -fill•ing] To <u>execute</u>: carry out; complete by performance. —ful•fill•er *n.*

and Webster's definition of "execute":

(*eks*-ih-kyoot) *v.* [ex•e•cut•ed; -cut'

1. To do; effect; carry out; complete. 2. <u>To enforce</u> put into effect. 3. To put to legally. 4. To make valid or legal. 5. To make or perform according to a pattern or design, as a work of art.—ex•e•cut•a•ble *adj.*

Do any of us want to be least in the kingdom of heaven? I think not, but most of the Christian world leans away from the fourth commandment, and some teach that keeping the Sabbath holy is not necessary. Those, according to the verses above, will be least in the kingdom of heaven. Sad. It doesn't say here that they won't be there, but let's see what more we can find.

> *Beware of false prophets, which come to you in sheep's clothing, but inwardly they are ravening wolves. Ye shall know them by their fruits. Do men gather grapes of thorns, or figs of thistles? Even so every good tree bringeth forth good fruit; but a corrupt tree bringeth forth evil fruit. A good tree cannot bring forth evil fruit, neither can a corrupt tree bring forth good fruit. Every tree that bringeth not forth good fruit is hewn down, and cast into the fire. Wherefore by their fruits ye shall know them.*

> *Not every one that saith unto me, Lord, Lord, shall enter into the kingdom of heaven; but he that doeth the will of my Father which is in heaven. Many will say to me in that day, Lord, Lord, have we not prophesied in thy name? And in thy name have cast out devils? And in thy name done many wonderful works? And then will I profess unto them, I never knew you: depart from me, ye that work iniquity.*

> *Therefore whosoever heareth these sayings of mine, and doeth them, I will liken him unto a wise man, which built his house upon a rock: and the rain descended, and the floods came, and the winds blew, and beat upon that house; and it fell not: for it was founded upon a rock. And every one that heareth these sayings of mine, and doeth them not, shall be likened unto a foolish man, which built his house upon the sand: and the rain descended, and the floods came, and the winds blew, and beat upon that*

house; and it fell: and great was the fall of it. (Matt. 7:15–27)

These next verses may reveal something you haven't considered before, especially verse eight. Check this out.

At that time Jesus went on the sabbath day through the corn; and his disciples were an hungered, and began to pluck the ears of corn and to eat. But when the Pharisees saw it, they said unto him, Behold, thy disciples do that which is not lawful to do upon the sabbath day. But he said unto them, Have ye not read what David did, when he was an hungered, and they that were with him; how he entered into the house of God, and did eat the shewbread, which was not lawful for him to eat, neither for them which were with him, but only for the priests? Or have ye not read in the law, how that on the sabbath days the priests in the temple profane the sabbath, and are blameless? But I say unto you, That in this place is one greater than the temple. But if ye had known what this meaneth, I will have mercy, and not sacrifice, ye would not have condemned the guiltless. For the Son of man is Lord even of the sabbath day." (Matt. 12:1–8)

> *For the Son of man is Lord even of the sabbath day*

Verse 8, *"For the Son of man is Lord even of the sabbath day."* Take note that it says *"is* Lord of the sabbath," not *was* Lord of the Sabbath, and if we believe that *"Jesus Christ the same yesterday, and to day, and for ever"* (Heb. 13:8) and *"For I am the* LORD, *I change not"* (Mal. 3:6), then we know that Jesus was, and is, and will be, the Lord of the Sabbath forever. Continue on with:

> *And when he was departed thence, he went into their synagogue: And, behold, there was a man which had his hand withered. And they asked him, saying, Is it lawful to heal on the sabbath days? that they might accuse him. And he said unto them, What man shall there be among you, that shall have one sheep, and if it fall into a pit on the sabbath day, will he not lay hold on it, and lift it out? How much then is a man better than a sheep? Wherefore it is lawful to do well on the sabbath days. (Matthew 12:9–12)*

Matthew 24:3–20 gives us a picture of what is to come upon this earth in the latter days of time. Verses 16–20 indicate that the Sabbath is still in effect at the end. It says,

> *Then let them which be in Judaea flee into the mountains: let him which is on the housetop not come down to take any thing out of his house: neither let him which is in the field return back to take his clothes. And woe unto them that are with child, and to them that give suck in those days! But pray ye that your flight be not in the winter, neither on the sabbath day. (Matt. 24:16–20)*

These next verses should really make us think. *"And he [Jesus] said unto them, The sabbath was made for man, and not man for the sabbath: Therefore the Son of man is Lord also of the sabbath" (Mark 2:27–28).*

Why would Jesus make the Sabbath for man? And if He is Lord of the Sabbath, and He never changes, why don't the Christian people of the world keep the Sabbath today? Is Jesus not our example?

And when the sabbath day was come, he began to teach in the synagogue: and many hearing him were astonished, saying, From whence hath this man these things? And what wisdom is this which is given unto him, that even such mighty works are wrought by his hands? (Mark 6:2)

How many times does it take, when it says Jesus taught in the synagogue or the temple on the Sabbath day, for us to realize that He was showing us an example of keeping the Sabbath?

And they went into Capernaum; and straightway on the sabbath day he [Jesus] entered into the synagogue, and taught. (Mark 1:21)

And he came to Nazareth, where he had been brought up: and, as his custom was, he went into the synagogue on the sabbath day, and stood up for to read. (Luke 4:16)

And came down to Capernaum, a city of Galilee, and taught them on the sabbath days. (Luke 4:31)

And it came to pass also on another sabbath, that he entered into the synagogue and taught. (Luke 6:6)

And he was teaching in one of the synagogues on the sabbath. (Luke 13:10)

The above verses were notes about Jesus Himself. Let's see how many more we can find about teaching and preaching on the Sabbath.

For they that dwell at Jerusalem, and their rulers, because they knew him not, nor yet the voices of the prophets which are read every sabbath day, they have fulfilled them in condemning him. (Acts 13:27)

And when the Jews were gone out of the synagogue, the Gentiles besought that these words might be preached to them the next sabbath. (Acts 13:42)

And the next sabbath day came almost the whole city together to hear the word of God. (Acts 13:44)

And on the sabbath we went out of the city by a river side, where prayer was wont to be made; and we sat down, and spake unto the women which resorted thither. (Acts 16:13)

And Paul, as his manner was, went in unto them, and three sabbath days reasoned with them out of the scriptures. (Acts 17:2)

And he [Paul] reasoned in the synagogue every sabbath, and persuaded the Jews and the Greeks. (Acts 18:4)

These verses show plainly that Jesus and His disciples after Him kept and taught the law and the Sabbath. It seems that Paul's writings have been used by many as a reason for not keeping the commandments and worshipping on Sunday instead of Saturday, the true Sabbath. But let's review a few verses of Paul's writings.

[Luke wrote,] And the day following Paul went in with us unto James; and all the elders were present. And when he had saluted them, he declared particularly what things God had wrought among the Gentiles by his ministry. And when they heard it, they glorified the Lord, and said unto him, Thou seest, brother, how many thousands of Jews there are which believe; and they are all zealous of the law: and they are informed of thee, that thou teachest all the Jews which are among the Gentiles to forsake Moses, saying that they ought not to circumcise their children, neither to walk after the customs. What is it therefore? The multitude must needs come together: for they will hear that thou art come. Do therefore this that we say to thee: we have four men which have a vow on them; them take, and purify thyself with them, and be at charges with them, that they may shave their heads: and all may know that those things, whereof they were informed concerning thee, are nothing; but that thou thyself also walkest orderly, and keepest the law. (Acts 21:18—24)

[Paul said,] But this I confess unto thee, that after the way which they call heresy, so worship I the God of my fathers, believing all things which are written in the law and in the prophets. (Acts 24:14)

[Paul wrote,] For as many as have sinned without law shall also perish without law: and as many as

have sinned in the law shall be judged by the law; <u>(for not the hearers of the law are just before God, but the doers of the law shall be justified</u>. (Rom. 2:12–13)

[Paul wrote,] For all have sinned, and come short of the glory of God; being justified freely by his grace through the redemption that is in Christ Jesus: whom God hath set forth to be a propitiation through faith in his blood, to declare his righteousness for the remission of sins that are past, through the forbearance of God; to declare, I say, at this time his righteousness: that he might be just, and the justifier of him which believeth in Jesus. Where is boasting then? It is excluded. By what law? Of works? Nay: but by the law of faith. Therefore we conclude that a man is justified by faith without the deeds of the law. Is he the God of the Jews only? Is he not also of the Gentiles? Yes, of the Gentiles also: seeing it is one God, which shall justify the circumcision by faith, and uncircumcision through faith. Do we then make void the law through faith? God forbid: yea, we establish the law. (Rom. 3:23–31)

These verses don't need much comment. They speak loud and clear that God's law and the holy Sabbath is as important today as it was since time began for man.

Do we have sin in the world today? Big time. What is the definition of sin? *"Whosoever commit-*

> *God's law and the holy Sabbath is as important today as it was since time began for man.*

teth sin transgresseth also the law: for sin is the transgression of the law" (1 John 3:4).

Now, what law do you suppose it's talking about?

Brethren, I write no new commandment unto you, but an old commandment which ye had from the beginning. the old commandment is the word which you have heard from the beginning. (1 John 2:7)

I rejoiced greatly that I found of thy children walking in truth, as we have received a commandment from the Father. And now I beseech thee, lady, not as though I wrote a new commandment unto thee, but that which we had from the beginning, that we love one another. And this is love, that we walk after his commandments. This is the commandment, that, as ye have heard from the beginning, ye should walk in it. (2 John 1:4–6)

What commandment did we have from the beginning?

And I will make thy seed to multiply as the stars of heaven, and will give unto thy seed all these countries; and in thy seed shall all the nations of the earth be blessed; because that Abraham obeyed my voice, and kept my charge, my commandments, my statutes, and my laws. (Gen. 26:4–5)

This is the first mention of laws in the Bible, so if God had laws in Abraham's time, He must have made them at Adam's time, because John said, *"The commandment, that, as ye have heard from the beginning."*

Adam was the beginning of humanity on this earth, so God's laws, the Ten Commandments written in stone for the Israelites, must have existed from the beginning.

Now, I know that in a number of places in Paul's writings, there are verses that might make some think that all of the Old Testament laws were abolished. But as we have already shown, by Paul's own words, that he himself kept the law.

And account that the longsuffering of our Lord is salvation; even as our beloved brother Paul also according to the wisdom given unto him hath written unto you; as also in all his epistles, speaking in them of these things; in which are some things hard to be understood, which they that are unlearned and unstable wrest, as they do also the other scriptures, unto their own destruction. (2 Peter 3:15–16)

And that from a child thou hast known the holy scriptures, which are able to make thee wise unto salvation through faith which is in Christ Jesus. All scripture is given by inspiration of God, and is profitable for doctrine, for reproof, for correction, for instruction in righteousness: that the man of God may be perfect, thoroughly furnished unto all good works. (2 Tim. 3:15–17)

All Scripture, of course, means the Old Testament as well as the New, and it was given to us for instruction and examples and encouragement to teach us God's ways. Let's use David's words in Psalms, for example. Almost the whole chapter has David's words and thoughts concerning God's law.

> *Blessed are the undefiled in the way, who walk in the law of the LORD. Blessed are they that keep his testimonies, and that seek him with the whole heart. They also do no iniquity: they walk in his ways. Thou hast commanded us to keep thy precepts diligently. O that my ways were directed to keep thy statutes! Then shall I not be ashamed, when I have respect unto all thy commandments. I will praise thee with uprightness of heart, when I shall have learned thy righteous judgments. I will keep thy statutes: O forsake me not utterly. (Ps. 119:1–8)*

Verse 2 says, *"Blessed are they that keep his testimonies."* Ever wonder exactly what he meant by keeping his testimonies? Mr. Webster's dictionary gives three definitions for its meaning, the first being "law."

Verse 4 says, *"Thou hast commanded us to keep thy precepts diligently."* Webster defines the word "precept" as a rule of action, or a guide to moral conduct.

Verse 5 says, *"O that my ways were directed to keep thy statutes!"* Webster defines the word "statute" as a written law.

It seems there's no way to get away from the fact that we should be keeping God's law.

Whosoever believeth that Jesus is the Christ is born of God: and every one that loveth him that begat loveth him also that is begotten of him. By this we know that we love the children of God, when we love God, and keep his commandments. For this is the love of God, that we keep his commandments: and his commandments are not grievous. (1 John 5:1–3)

There are several places, as you have already read, where, when the law is mentioned, some of the Ten Commandments are quoted, showing us exactly what law is being spoken of.

> *It seems there's no way to get away from the fact that we should be keeping God's law.*

Jesus himself quoted the commandments more than once when He was asked what one needed to do to be saved, and if Jesus spoke it, I, for one, will do my best, with a lot of prayer and God's help, to keep those commandments.

God works in mysterious ways. A few days ago, I was sorting through some old files from many years ago and found a small pocket tablet where I had made notes for my work from time to time. In thumbing through it, I came across a couple of pages of verses I had jotted down while listening to a sermon at church forty-two years ago. I took those pages out and would like to share some of the verses with you.

If any of you lack wisdom, let him ask of God, that giveth to all men liberally, and upbraideth not; and it shall be given him. (James 1:5)

And whatsoever we ask, we receive of him, because we keep his commandments, and do those things that are pleasing in his sight. (1 John 3:22)

If ye keep my commandments, ye shall abide in my love; even as I have kept my Father's commandments, and abide in his love. (John 15:10)

For even hereunto were ye called: because Christ also suffered for us, leaving us an example, that ye should follow his steps. (1 Peter 2:21)

And that day was the preparation, and the sabbath drew on. And the women also, which came with him from Galilee, followed after, and beheld the sepulcher, and how his body was laid. And they returned, and prepared spices and ointments; and rested the sabbath day according to the commandment. (Luke 23:54–56)

Here we see that after Jesus's death His commandments were still kept, and if He is our example, and He kept the Sabbath, and He was Lord of the Sabbath, and He never changes, how can we deny that we should be keeping His commandments today?

"The sabbath was made for man" (Mark 2:27–28). Why would He make the Sabbath for man? He showed us that when He finished the creation of this earth and its contents. He rested on the seventh day and blessed it, and made it holy and gave it to us for a day of worship and rest.

> *Let us therefore fear, lest, a promise being left us of entering into his rest, any of you should seem to come short of it. For unto us was the gospel preached, as well as unto them: but the word preached did not profit them, not being mixed with faith in them that heard it. For we which have believed do enter into rest, as he said, As I have sworn in my wrath, if they shall enter into my rest: although the works were finished from the foundation of the world. For he spake in a certain place of the seventh day on this wise, And God did rest the seventh day from all his works. And in this place again, If they shall enter into my rest. Seeing therefore it remaineth that some must enter therein, and they to whom it was first preached entered not in because of unbelief. Again, he limiteth a certain day, saying in David, To day, after so long a time; as it is said, <u>To day, if ye will hear his voice, harden not your hearts. For if Jesus had given them rest, then would he not afterward have spoken of another day. There remaineth therefore a rest to the people of God. For he that is entered into his rest, he also hath ceased from his own works. as God did from his. Let us labour therefore to enter into that rest, lest any man fall after the same example of unbelief.</u> (Heb. 4:1–11)*

Here Paul tells us in no uncertain terms, that the seventh day is God's day of rest. Verse three says "we which have believed do enter into rest," showing they were keeping the Sabbath as God directed.

I'm eighty years old as I write these words, and I have been blessed with more work than I could do for most of my working years. I look forward to every Sabbath for the rest of body and mind. At this age, the Sabbath gets more important to me, and Jesus gets more important to me. As the body ages and the strength declines, so the Sabbath of rest is very much looked forward to. Just a few more verses:

> *Whosoever believeth that Jesus is the Christ is born of God: and every one that loveth him that begat loveth him also that is begotten of him. By this we know that we love the children of God, when we love God, and keep his commandments. For this is the love of God, that we keep his commandments: and his commandments are not grievous. (1 John 5:1–3)*

> *And the dragon was wroth with the woman, and went to make war with the remnant of her seed, which keep the commandments of God, and have the testimony of Jesus Christ. (Rev. 12:17)*

> *Here is the patience of the saints: here are they that keep the commandments of God, and the faith of Jesus. (Rev. 14:12)*

> *Blessed are they that do his commandments, that they may have right to the tree of life, and may enter in through the gates into the city. (Rev. 22:14)*

> *For I testify unto every man that heareth the words of the prophecy of this book, if any man shall add unto these things, God shall add unto him the plagues that are written in this book: and if any man shall take*

away from the words of the book of this prophecy, God shall take away his part out of the book of life, and out of the holy city, and from the things which are written in this book. (Rev. 22:18–19)

I hesitate to write my thoughts on those verses, yet I feel I should make a point here. Most of the Christian world believes we should keep God's Ten Commandments and keep Sunday as a holy day. In so doing, they are taking away from God's Word by ignoring the fourth of the Ten Commandments.

I need also to say that my thoughts and beliefs written here are not written to criticize, or offend, or to disagree with anyone. I'm writing to encourage people to study and be approved, as it says, *"Study to shew thyself approved unto God, a workman that needeth not to be ashamed, rightly dividing the word of truth" (2 Tim. 2:15).*

Earlier, I mentioned I had taken Bible studies sent to me by mail that helped me to determine to keep the Sabbath. I would like to share with you some writings from "The Good News about God's Unchangeable Day" from issue #12 of *Good News for Today*.

> *Most of the Christian world believes we should keep God's Ten Commandments and keep Sunday as a holy day. In so doing, they are taking away from God's Word by ignoring the fourth of the Ten Commandments.*

Question: *"What do spokesmen for other churches say about the change of the Sabbath as a holy day of worship?"*

Answer: *Our Catholic friends say*: "You may read the Bible from Genesis to Revelation, and you will not find a single line authorizing the sanctification of Sunday. The Scriptures enforce the religious observance of Saturday." —*The Faith of Our Fathers*, p. 89.

Our Episcopalian friends say: "The Bible commandment says on the seventh day thou shalt rest. That is Saturday. Nowhere in the Bible is it laid down that worship should be done on Sunday." —Toronto *Daily Star*, Oct. 26, 1949.

Our Lutheran friends declare: "The observance of the Lord's day [Sunday] is founded not on any command by God, but on the authority of the church." —Augsburg Confession of Faith," quoted in *Cox's Sabbath Manual*, p. 287.

Others acknowledge the change: "The notion of a formal substitution by apostolic authority of the Lord's Day [Sunday] for the Jewish Sabbath ... has no basis whatever, either in Holy Scripture or in Christian antiquity." —*Dictionary of Christian Antiquities*. Vol. 2, p. 182.

History records the change: "Not long after the recognition of Christianity by Constantine, the observance of Sunday was required by law. In AD 321, all courts of justice, all city dwellers and artisans were required to rest 'on the venerable day of the sun.'" —*Encyclopedia Americana* (1969), Vol. XXVI, p. 32.

When Constantine's famous Sunday law was promulgated, he did not call Sunday the Lord's Day, but the "venerable day of the sun." He was enforcing not a Christian institution but a pagan custom. By forcing the heathen festival of Sunday upon Christians, he hoped to bring about a fusion of paganism and Christianity, thus uniting his kingdom. But what began as a pagan ordinance ended as a Christian regulation, and a long series of imperial decrees during the fourth, fifth, and sixth centuries enjoined with increasing stringency abstinence from labor on Sunday.

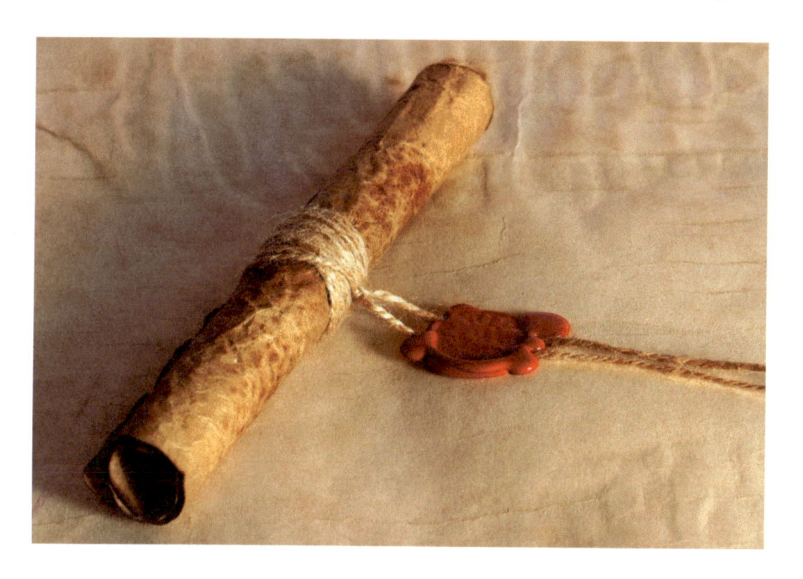

The church at Rome accepted many teachings that were not found in the Bible. It had put its seal of approval on the change of the day of worship and commanded everyone to keep Sunday as the holy day instead of Saturday. Notice the following quotation from the *Convert's Catechism of Catholic Doctrine*, p. 50:

"**Q.** Which is the Sabbath day?"
"**A.** Saturday is the Sabbath day."

"**Q.** Why do we observe Sunday instead of Saturday?"
"**A.** We observe Sunday instead of Saturday because the Catholic Church transferred the solemnity from Saturday to Sunday."

Q. *What challenge is given by Catholics to Protestants concerning the change of the day of worship?*

A. "The church changed the observance of the Sabbath to Sunday by right of the divine, infallible authority given to her by her Founder, Jesus Christ. The Protestant, claiming the Bible to be the only guide of faith, has no warrant for observing Sunday."—*The Catholic Universe Bulletin*, Aug. 14, 1942.

"You are a Protestant, and you profess to go by the Bible and the Bible only; and yet in so important a matter as the observance of one day in seven as a holy day, you go against the plain letter of the Bible, and put another day in the place of that day which the Bible has commanded." —*Library of Christian Doctrine*, p. 3.

Did God direct anyone to change the Sabbath to Sunday? Peter said "We ought to obey God rather than men" *(Acts 5:29).*

And I have read the Bible through many times and have even hoped to find that the Sabbath was changed to Sunday. But it's simply not there anywhere. The truth is made clear how and when it was changed—yet most of the Christian people of the world worship on the first day of the week instead of the true seventh-day Sabbath. I wish I could understand why.

Now, I would like to add something to encourage each one to not delay in accepting Jesus, if you haven't already. Time is running out.

> *And as he [Jesus] sat upon the mount of Olives, the disciples came unto him privately, saying, Tell us, when shall these things be? and what shall be the sign of thy coming, and of the end of the world?*
>
> *And Jesus answered and said unto them, Take heed that no man deceive you. For many shall come in my*

name, saying, I am Christ; and shall deceive many. And ye shall hear of wars and rumours of wars: see that ye be not troubled: for all these things must come to pass, but the end is not yet. For nation shall rise against nation, and kingdom against kingdom: and there shall be famines, and pestilences, and earthquakes, in divers places. All these are the beginning of sorrows. Then shall they deliver you up to be afflicted, and shall kill you: and ye shall be hated of all nations for my name's sake. And then shall many be offended, and shall betray one another, and shall hate one another. And many false prophets shall rise, and shall deceive many. And because iniquity shall abound, the love of many shall wax cold. But he that shall endure unto the end, the same shall be saved.

And this gospel of the kingdom shall be preached in all the world for a witness unto all nations; and then shall the end come. When ye therefore shall see the abomination of desolation, spoken of by Daniel the prophet, stand in the holy place, (whoso readeth, let him understand:) Then let them which be in Judaea flee into the mountains: Let him which is on the housetop not come down to take any thing out of his house: Neither let him which is in the field return back to take his clothes. And woe

> **And this gospel of the kingdom shall be preached in all the world for a witness unto all nations; and then shall the end come.**

unto them that are with child, and to them that give suck in those days!

But pray ye that your flight be not in the winter, neither on the sabbath day: For then shall be great tribulation, such as was not since the beginning of the world to this time, no, nor ever shall be. And except those days should be shortened, there should no flesh be saved: but for the elect's sake those days shall be shortened. Then if any man shall say unto you, Lo, here is Christ, or there; believe it not. For there shall arise false Christs, and false prophets, and shall shew great signs and wonders; insomuch that, if it were possible, they shall deceive the very elect. Behold, I have told you before. Wherefore if they shall say unto you, Behold, he is in the desert; go not forth: behold, he is in the secret chambers; believe it not. For as the lightning cometh out of the east, and shineth even unto the west; so shall also the coming of the Son of man be. For wheresoever the carcass is, there will the eagles be gathered together.

Immediately after the tribulation those days shall the sun be darkened, and the moon shall not give her light, and the stars shall fall from heaven, and the powers of the heavens shall be shaken: And then shall appear the sign of the Son of man in heaven: and then shall all the tribes of the earth mourn, and they shall see the Son of man coming in the clouds of heaven with power and great glory. And he shall send his angels with a great sound of a trumpet, and they shall gather together his elect from the four winds, from one end of heaven to the other. Now learn a parable of the fig free; When his branch is yet tender, and putteth forth leaves, ye know that summer is nigh: So likewise ye, when ye shall see all these things, know that it is near, even at the doors. Verily I say unto you, this generation shall not pass, till all these things be fulfilled. Heaven and earth shall pass away, but my words shall not pass away. But of that day and hour knoweth no man, no, not the angels of heaven, but my Father only.

But as the days of Noah were, so shall also the coming of the Son of man be. For as in the days that were before the flood they were eating and drinking, marrying and giving in marriage, until the day that Noe entered into the ark, And knew not until the flood came, and took them all away; so shall also the coming of the Son of man be. Then shall two be in the field; the one shall be taken, and the other left. Two women shall be grinding at the mill; the one shall be taken, and the other left.

Watch therefore: for ye know not what hour your Lord doth come. But know this, that if the goodman of the house had known in what watch the thief would come, he would have watched, and would not have suffered his house to be broken up. Therefore be ye also ready: for in such an hour as ye think not the Son of man cometh." (Matt. 24:3–44)

Here, Jesus Himself has given us the information we need, so we can know when the time of His coming is near. Are we seeing any of these things happening today? I think we are, big time! *"But thou, O Daniel, shut up the words, and seal the book, even to the time of the end: many shall run to and fro, and knowledge shall be increased"* (Dan. 12:4).

Ever get in a traffic jam and wish you would have stayed at home? There is a lot of running to and fro out there today. And increased knowledge? Wow! Just think what has changed in the last hundred years because of increased knowledge. It's almost unbelievable the things that people have accomplished.

And there is one point in particular I would like to make from *Matthew 24:34*. Jesus said, *"Verily I say unto you, this generation shall not pass, till all these things be fulfilled."*

I believe we could be in that generation now, with all the things happening in this world that Jesus spoke of in Matthew 24. We don't know exactly when that generation may have started, but if seventy years is the average generation, or eighty, or even a hundred, it could be well on its way to being over now.

God bless you as you read and pray over these words from God's Word.

And now as I come to an end of these studies, I appeal to you, friends, family, and brothers and sisters of all faiths. Pray and take to heart the things you have read in these verses from God's Word. Follow the example of Jesus Himself as He walked the earth and taught us to love one another, to keep His laws, and to rest and worship Him on His Sabbath days that He gave us from the beginning.

Turn away from the traditions of humanity and follow the ways of God.

For God so loved the world, that he gave his only begotten Son, that whoesoever believeth in him should not perish, but have everlasting life. (John 3:16)

This is God's remedy for our sins. Praise God for His love and mercy.

—Al Matlock

Food for thought...

Think about this: "Why do I worship on Sunday, the first day of the week, instead of Saturday, the seventh day, as God directed?"

And hereby we do know that we know him, if we keep his commandments. He that saith, I know him, and keepeth not his commandments, is a liar, and the truth is not in him. (1 John 2:3, 4)

Ask yourself, "Do I keep God's commandment—*all of them*—or would God consider me a liar?"

More Food for thought...

In this book there are over 250 verses all indicating that we should be keeping the Ten Commandments and the seventh-day Sabbath. There is not one verse in the whole bible that directs us to worship on Sunday.